T0163145

THE
UNDERSTANDING
YOUR GRIEF

Journal

[SECOND EDITION]

ALSO BY ALAN WOLFELT

Understanding Your Grief:
Ten Essential Touchstones for Finding Hope
and Healing Your Heart

Companioning the Bereaved:
A Soulful Guide for Caregivers

Healing Your Grieving Heart:
100 Practical Ideas

Grief One Day at a Time:
365 Meditations to Help You Heal After Loss

Healing a Parent's Grieving Heart:
100 Practical Ideas After Your Child Dies

The Journey Through Grief:
Reflections On Healing

Loving from the Outside In,
Mourning from the Inside Out

Companion
P R E S S

Companion Press is dedicated to the education and support
of both the bereaved and bereavement caregivers. We believe that those
who companion the bereaved by walking with them as they journey in
grief have a wondrous opportunity: to help others embrace and
grow through grief—and to lead fuller, more deeply-lived lives
themselves because of this important ministry.

For a complete catalog and ordering information, write or call:

Companion Press
The Center for Loss and Life Transition
3735 Broken Bow Road
Fort Collins, CO 80526
(970) 226-6050
www.centerforloss.com

THE UNDERSTANDING YOUR GRIEF

Journal

EXPLORING THE TEN ESSENTIAL TOUCHSTONES

[SECOND EDITION]

ALAN D. WOLFELT, PH.D.

Companion
PRESS

Fort Collins, Colorado
An imprint of the Center for Loss and Life Transition

First edition, ISBN 978-1-879651-39-5 © 2004 by Alan D. Wolfelt, Ph.D.

Second edition, ISBN 978-1-61722-309-9 © 2021 by Alan D. Wolfelt, Ph.D.

All rights reserved. No part of this publication may be reproduced, stored in a retrieval system, or transmitted in any form or by any means, electronic, mechanical, photocopying, recording, or otherwise, without the prior permission of the publisher.

Companion Press is an imprint of the
Center for Loss and Life Transition
3735 Broken Bow Road
Fort Collins, Colorado 80526

Printed in the United States of America

30   29   28   27   26   25   24   5   4

ISBN: 978-1-61722-309-9

The *Understanding Your Grief* Series

SECOND EDITION

This book is designed to be used along with *Understanding Your Grief, Second Edition*, also by Dr. Alan Wolfelt. There is also a support group faciliator guide available entitled *The Understanding Your Grief Support Group Guide, Second Edition*.

There is also a daily reader version titled *365 Days of Understanding your Grief*. This text serves as ideal supplemental reading for the griever.

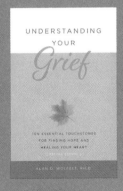

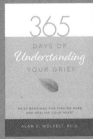

Contents

Introduction

This guided journal is a companion to the second edition of my book *Understanding Your Grief: Ten Essential Touchstones for Finding Hope and Healing Your Heart.* I hope it can be a safe place for you to explore your grief and your experience with the ten essential touchstones.

> "Writing is the most profound way of codifying your thoughts, the best way of learning from yourself who you are and what you believe."
>
> Warren Bennis

The difference between a blank notebook and a guided journal is that a guided journal asks you questions and invites you to respond. This friendly structure makes it easier for many grieving people to write down their thoughts and feelings. It helps them tell their story in short, doable bits and pieces. It also helps them more deeply engage with and internalize the content of *Understanding Your Grief.* I hope this is the case for you, too.

As you tell your story, your words will guide you on your unique journey through the wilderness of your grief. Your words will also give testimony to the love you will always have for the person who died. You can use the journal not only to understand your grief but to remember, celebrate, and honor the life of the person to whom you dedicate this journal.

The Value of Grief Journaling

Journaling has proven to be an excellent way for many people to do the work of mourning. Journaling is private and independent, yet it's still expressing your grief outside of yourself. I've been a grief counselor for a long time now (nearly forty years!), and I've found that while it may not be for everyone, the process of putting the written word on paper is profoundly helpful to many grieving people in the following ways:

Grief journaling...

• honors the person who died.

• clarifies what you're thinking and feeling.

• offers a safe place of solace—a place where you can fully express yourself no matter what you're experiencing.

• allows you to tap into the touchstones of the companion book.

• helps soften the intensity of your thoughts and feelings.

• helps you better understand both your grief and your mourning.

• clears out your naturally overwhelmed mind and heart.

• examines the pain you are experiencing and transforms it into something survivable.

• creates an opportunity to acknowledge the balance in your life between the sad and the happy.

• strengthens your awareness of how your grief journey changes over time.

• maps out your transformation as you journey through grief.

As one author observed, "When you write, you lay out a line of words. The line of words is a miner's pick, a woodcarver's gouge, a surgeon's probe. You wield it, and it digs a path you follow." To this I would add that a grief journal can provide a lifeline when you are in the midst of the wilderness. As you learn, mourn, and discover, you can and will reach the destination of this path—reconciliation.

Journaling Suggestions

First, please remember that there is no "right" way to use this journal. You will not be graded on how quickly you complete the pages that follow. Actually, I would suggest that you take your time. If you are using this resource as part of a support group experience, your leaders will probably have you fill out the journal one chapter at a time over the course of weeks or months, effectively dosing your journaling experience.

If you're reading the second edition of *Understanding Your Grief* and completing this journal on your own, I suggest you find a trusted person who can be available to you if and when you want to talk out any thoughts and feelings the journal brings up for you. When I say a trusted person, I mean someone who accepts you where you are right now in your grief journey. This person shouldn't judge you or think it's their job to get you "over" your grief quickly. Remember— you don't "get over" grief, and there are no rewards for speed!

You will notice that in addition to the guided journal sections, in which you are asked to answer specific questions about your unique grief journey, there are a number of "Notes" pages throughout this book. These are places for you to freely write about whatever is on your heart as you are completing the journal. At the end of the journal, you will also find a section entitled "Continuing Your Journey." This is a place to write down your ongoing thoughts and feelings about the death after you've completed the journal—in the months and years to come.

SETTING

Pick a safe place to write in your journal. Naturally, journaling is usually easier to do in a quiet place that is free from interruptions and distractions. Consider setting aside your phone and other electronics for a few minutes and allowing your mind and heart to be fully present to your grief.

HONESTY

If an effort to open yourself to your grief and mourning, you must be honest with yourself. You must think your true thoughts and write them out, feel your genuine feelings and express them.

PRIVACY

This is your journal and yours alone. Remember—you don't have to share or show it to anyone you don't want to. If you're participating in a grief support group, you may be invited to share some of what you write in your journal. This can be a very helpful thing to do, but sharing should always be optional, not mandatory.

Be Gentle with Yourself

Some people shy away from writing in a journal because they don't think they're good writers. Actually, it doesn't matter in the least if you're a "good writer" or not, at least in the English-teacher sense of that term. The point isn't to test your vocabulary or your grammar or even your creative writing skills but rather to explore what's on your mind and in your heart. Don't judge or criticize what you find comes to paper. Ignore your penmanship and don't worry about punctuation or spelling. This journal is for you. Journaling is a breathing space on paper. Breathe deep and go forth!

A journal is a confessor. It simply listens as you write. Believe in your ability to set your intention to integrate this loss into your life. I'm honored that you are using this resource as one instrument to help you come out of the dark and into the light.

I hope we cross paths one day.

Alan D. Wolfelt

Dedication

I dedicate this journal in memory of

_____

(name of the person who died)

_____

(your name)

_____

(your relationship to the person who died)

Place a photograph below of your special person who died:

This photo is meaningful to me because

_____

_____

_____

_____

An Invitation to Open Your Heart

This guided journal is a safe place for you to express your many thoughts, feelings, and memories. Its purpose is to help you grow to understand your grief and become friends with it. It's intended to help you open your heart and explore how the death of someone loved is changing your life. My hope is that it will not only help provide you some much-deserved support, it will also honor your relationship with someone who has been a special part of your life here on earth.

"Surrounded by my memories, I took my pen and began to write."

Kuki Gallmann

Before you begin this journal experience, please take a few minutes to reflect on where you are right now in your grief journey.

INTRODUCTION TO
Understanding Your Grief

In this chapter in the companion text...

We began to consider that grief is something that needs your attention. We acknowledged that understanding grief is a paradox—that you must also learn to surrender to the mysteries of life and death. You were introduced to the ten touchstones, which are essential signs to look for in the wilderness of your grief. You were encouraged to foster hope and remember that healing in grief is heart-based, not head-based. This is because grief is first and foremost a spiritual journey and demands a search for meaning. You were encouraged to own your rightful role as expert of your grief experience. And you were invited to fill out this journal as a way to do the healing work of mourning.

UNDERSTANDING AS SURRENDERING

Understanding the basic principles of grief and mourning helps people on their journeys. But surrendering to the mysteries of life and death that cannot be fully explained is also necessary.

As you begin this journal, how are you feeling about learning to understand your grief and also, at the same time, surrendering to the reality that we as human beings cannot fully comprehend all the mysteries of life and death?

THE TEN TOUCHSTONES

The ten touchstones are the essential physical, cognitive, emotional, social, and spiritual signs to seek out in your grief journey. They are your trail markers. They let you know you are on the right path.

As you embark on this journaling experience, how are you feeling about the ten touchstones? Which are you most curious about? Which seem scary to you?

FINDING HOPE

Hope is an expectation of a good that is yet to be. It's a future-looking expectation felt in the present moment. How are your hope levels right now? What are you hopeful about? If you are struggling with hope right now, why do you think this is?

HEALING YOUR HEART

Even though the term "understanding" is used in the title of the companion book, grief is more a journey of the heart and soul than it is a path toward cognitive understanding and acceptance. Are you someone who is generally more inclined to feel than think, or think than feel? Please share a little about your head, your heart, and your courage.

A WORD ABOUT FAITH AND SPIRITUALITY

Grief is a spiritual journey because the death of someone loved forces us to examine our most fundamental beliefs and feelings about why we are here and what life means. Please share a little here about your own religious or spiritual background. Also, how has this death affected your religious or spiritual beliefs and practices?

OWNING AND HONORING YOUR JOURNEY

Your grief is yours. You and only you can be the expert of your own grief experience. Up to this point, have you felt confident or unconfident (or somewhere in the middle) about "owning" your grief? Please explain.

HOW TO USE THIS BOOK

Journaling about your grief is a powerful method for helping yourself heal. Some people dive right into journaling, and others are more hesitant. How are you feeling about answering the questions in this guided journal and using journaling as a tool for mourning?

Open to the Presence of Your Loss

In this chapter in the companion text...

We discussed the necessity of opening to the presence of your loss. To heal in grief, you must honor—not avoid—the pain. One way to embrace the pain while at the same time maintaining hope for the future is by setting your intention to heal. Even as you embrace your pain and set your intention to heal, remember that healing in grief does not happen quickly or efficiently. Also remember that the common perception of "doing well" in grief is erroneous. To "do well" with your grief, you must not be strong and silent but rather mourn openly and honestly.

As you were reading *Understanding Your Grief*, you discovered that honoring your grief means, in part, "recognizing the value of and respecting." Describe any ways in which you have honored your grief.

The pain of your grief will keep trying to get your attention until you have the courage to gently, and in small doses, open to its presence. How is the pain of your grief trying to get your attention?

What does it mean to you to gently "dose" yourself with the pain of your grief?

SETTING YOUR INTENTION TO HEAL

You learned that when you set your intention to heal, you make a true commitment to positively influence the course of your journey. Use the space below to explore your intention to heal in grief.

When you set your intention to heal, you choose between being what I call a "passive witness" to your grief or an "active participant" in your grief. Describe below your understanding of the difference between being a "passive witness" versus an "active participant" in your grief.

MAKING GRIEF YOUR FRIEND

"Even as I mourn, I can continue to love." Do you agree with this statement? Why or why not?

_____

_____

_____

_____

_____

_____

_____

_____

NO REWARDS FOR SPEED

Reconciling your grief does not happen quickly or efficiently. How do you feel about your capacity to go slow and be patient with yourself in your journey through grief?

_____

_____

_____

_____

_____

_____

_____

_____

"DOING WELL" WITH YOUR GRIEF

Sometimes people who are openly mourning feel ashamed of their thoughts, feelings, and behaviors. Do you feel any sense of shame or embarrassment about how your grief feels or how you are mourning? If so, write about it below.

THE IMPORTANCE OF PRESENCE

To be present is to notice and give attention to whatever is happening around you and inside you in each moment. It is to honor and mindfully experience the now. Your grief needs your presence. How are you doing so far at being present to your grief?

GRIEF IS NOT A DISEASE

Grief is not a disease—it is a normal part of love. While grief is a powerful experience, so, too, is your capacity to aid your own healing. Write about any steps you've taken (even baby steps!) to help yourself begin to heal.

Dispel a Dozen Misconceptions about Grief

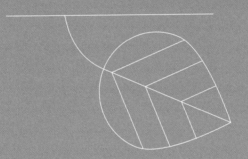

In this chapter in the companion text...

We discovered that many of the perceptions we may have had—and society often teaches us—about grief and mourning aren't true at all. For example, grief does NOT progress in predictable, orderly stages. And tears aren't a sign of weakness; actually, they're a form of mourning, and they are natural and normal. Many misconceptions color our expectations about grief. The trick is to sort out the fact from the fiction and grieve and mourn in healthy, authentic ways.

MISCONCEPTION 1:
Grief and mourning are the same thing

Did you used to think that grief and mourning were the same thing? If so, how has this misconception affected you?

Now that we've explored the difference between grief and mourning, how will you mourn this death by openly and honestly expressing your grief outside of yourself?

Do you see yourself having difficulty with expressing your grief outside of yourself (mourning) in any ways? If so, how?

MISCONCEPTION 2:

Grief and mourning progress in predictable, orderly stages

Have you heard about the "stages of grief"? If so, what is or was your feeling about this popular grief model?

_____

_____

_____

_____

_____

_____

_____

_____

_____

Now that you've learned that "stages" in grief aren't orderly or predictable, how do you believe you will move forward in your own unique journey through grief?

_____

_____

_____

_____

_____

Grief is often a one step forward, two steps back process. How could you help yourself during those inevitable times when you feel stuck in your grief?

MISCONCEPTION 3:

You should move away from grief, not toward it

Have you felt pressured to "overcome" your grief instead of experiencing it? If so, how and why have you been pressured?

What does it mean to you to move toward your pain?

How could you deal with friends, family, coworkers, etc. who encourage you (either outright or implicitly) to move away from your grief?

MISCONCEPTION 4:

Tears of grief are a sign of weakness

Have you cried since the death? If so, in what circumstances and how often? If not, why not?

_____

_____

_____

_____

_____

_____

_____

_____

Do others around you make you feel a sense of shame or weakness about crying? If so, who and why?

_____

_____

_____

_____

_____

_____

_____

Do you yourself feel a sense of shame or weakness about crying?
If so, what can you do to help yourself understand that tears can be a
normal form of mourning?

MISCONCEPTION 5:

Being upset and openly mourning means you are being "weak" in your faith

Are you a person of faith? Do you believe in God or a power greater than yourself? Whether your answer is yes or no, please write about your personal beliefs.

Do you think you are being weak in your faith if you are struggling with this death? Or has anyone else made you feel this way? Write about your understanding of the relationship between healthy mourning and having faith.

MISCONCEPTION 6:

When someone you love dies, you only grieve and mourn for the physical absence of the person

Since the death, you may have realized that there are many things you have lost besides the company of the person who died. List the "ripple-effect" losses you are experiencing as a result of the death.

From the above list, choose one or two of your most hurtful or significant "ripple-effect" losses and write about them here.

MISCONCEPTION 7:

You should try not to think about the person who died on special days like holidays, anniversaries, and birthdays

Have you encountered a holiday, anniversary, or birthday since the death that was connected to the person who died? Describe what you did on this day and how you felt.

_____

_____

_____

_____

_____

_____

_____

_____

_____

On this day, did you try to avoid thinking about the person who died, or did you try to honor your grief and the memory of the person who died? Write about your choice and how it turned out for you.

_____

_____

_____

_____

What is the next upcoming special day where you will probably especially feel the absence of the person who died? How could you commemorate their life and your continuing love for them on this day?

MISCONCEPTION 8:

At the funeral or as soon as possible, you have to say goodbye to the person who died

Before reading *Understanding Your Grief*, what was your understanding of the funeral as "closure"?

_____

_____

_____

_____

_____

_____

_____

_____

_____

The funeral and the early days and weeks of grief are more about saying hello to the reality of the death than they are about saying goodbye. They are more a time of opening than of closure.

Where are you right now in the process of saying hello to various aspects of your life today?

_____

_____

_____

_____

Where are you right now in the process of saying goodbye to the person who died and to different aspects of your life as it was before?

MISCONCEPTION 9:

After someone you love dies, the goal should be to "get over" your grief as soon as possible

Had you been hoping to "get over" your grief? If so, why? If not, why not?

Has anyone else told you or made you feel that you need to "get over" your grief? If so, who and in what circumstances? How did this make you feel?

How do you feel about the reality that you will not "get over" your grief but rather learn to reconcile yourself to it?

MISCONCEPTION 10:
Nobody can help you with your grief

Are you normally an independent person who does everything for yourself, or are you an interdependent person who relies on others for help with some things? Explain.

In order to heal, you will need to reach out to others to help you with your grief. Do you believe this to be true? Why or why not?

List at least three people who would be naturally good companions for you on your journey through the wilderness of your grief.

MISCONCEPTION 11:

If you're focusing too much on your grief, you're being selfish

Have you ever felt weak, selfish, or self-indulgent in your grief—or have others suggested that you should feel this way for focusing on your grief? If so, when and why?

Acknowledging, being present to, befriending, expressing, and even appropriately wallowing in your grief are essential for you right now. What tasks, obligations, and beliefs in your life are competing with the need to make your grief and mourning a top priority?

If you became aware that you're not giving your grief as much attention as it deserves, what are some ways that you could carve out more time and energy to attend to and actively mourn your grief?

MISCONCEPTION 12:

When grief and mourning are finally reconciled, they never come up again

This misconception is a close cousin to Misconception 9, which says that your goal should be to "get over" your grief as soon as possible. Grief doesn't end, but it does erupt less frequently. Have you had any recent "eruptions" you could write about?

Do you have any "grief role models" in your life—people who mourned openly and honestly after a death and went on to reconcile their grief and continue to live a life of meaning and joy? If so, who? How does this person (or these people) continue to acknowledge and honor their grief and ongoing love in the years and decades after the death?

Use the space below to write out any additional misconceptions you have experienced or observed and the ways in which they have thus far influenced your grief journey.

Realistic Expectations For Grief and Mourning

Please write just a few words in response to each of these truths:

1. Grief is internal. Mourning is external. You will naturally grieve, but you will probably have to make a conscious, intentional, and regular effort to mourn.

2. Your grief will be unpredictable, and it will not likely progress in an orderly fashion. What's more, it will involve a wide variety of different thoughts and feelings.

3. You must welcome your grief and make it your friend. You need to feel it to heal it. Also, even as you're working to befriend your grief, it will probably hurt more before it hurts less.

4. Crying and all forms of expression of grief and mourning are signs of strength.

5. Having faith and experiencing deep grief can go hand-in-hand.

6. When someone you love dies, you not only suffer the loss of their physical presence, you also experience any number of secondary losses. Your grief and mourning will impact you in all five realms of experience: physically, cognitively, emotionally, socially, and spiritually.

7. Special days like holidays, anniversaries, and birthdays naturally arouse your grief and are excellent times to mourn openly and seek support from others.

8. You have to say "hello" to your grief and all of your thoughts and feelings of loss—a process that takes a long time—before you can begin to find ways to say goodbye to the chapter of your life that is now over.

9. You will never "get over" your grief. Instead, you will learn to live with it.

10. You need other people to help you with and through your grief. You must accept their support, and you must also reach out for support.

11. Spending time and energy focusing on and expressing your grief is essential self-care. It's hard, necessary work.

12. You will always grieve for the person who died, and you will probably experience griefbursts forever. But if you mourn openly and thoroughly in doses for as long as it takes, your grief will soften over time. You will not always feel this bad.

NOTES

Embrace the
Uniqueness of Your Grief

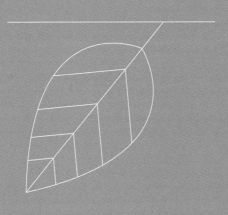

In this chapter in the companion text...

We developed an understanding that each person's grief is unique and that grief and mourning can never be strictly compared. We also explored all the many reasons that your grief is your grief—why it is unique to you and unlike anyone else's.

WHY 1:

Your Relationship with the Person Who Died

If someone asked you to describe your relationship with the person who died, what would immediately come to your mind and heart?

_____

_____

_____

_____

_____

_____

_____

_____

How attached were you to this person?

_____

_____

_____

_____

_____

Describe how you acted and felt in one another's company.

Can you remember a time when you felt very close to this person? Please describe it here.

Were there times when it was difficult to get along with this person? If so, give some examples of those times. If not, write about why you think you got along so well.

What did the person who died look like?

Approximate height _____ Approximate weight _____

Hair color and type _____ Eye color _____

Other distinguishing characteristics:

Write about two special memories you will always have of your relationship with the person who died.

WHY 2:

The Circumstances of the Death

Describe the circumstances of the death.

How did you learn about the death?

Was the death something you expected to happen, or was it sudden and unexpected? How does the answer to this question affect your grief?

_____

_____

_____

_____

_____

_____

_____

_____

_____

_____

How old was the person who died? _____

Is the person's age affecting your grief? If so, how?

_____

_____

_____

_____

_____

_____

What questions, if any, do you still have about how or why the person died?

Is there someone you could talk to who could help work these questions out?

What other thoughts and feelings come to mind when you think about how this person died?

WHY 3:

The People in Your Life

Do you have people in your life (friends and family) whom you can turn to for help and support during your time of grief? Who? List them.

_____

_____

_____

_____

What qualities do these people have that make them able to walk with you in your grief?

_____

_____

_____

_____

Are there people in your life you might be able to turn to for support but feel like you can't? If so, who and why?

_____

_____

_____

_____

_____

_____

_____

Are you willing to accept support from friends and family? If so, why? If not, why not?

The pressure-cooker phenomenon is when several people in the same family or friend group are all grieving the death and so have a naturally limited capacity to support one another. Has this happened to you, and if so, who else could you turn to for grief support?

What are some things that people have said or done that have been helpful to you?

Do you have friends at work, at your place of worship, and/or at an organization you are a part of who are supportive of your grief?
☐ Yes ☐ No

Who are these people, and how can you continue to reach out to them?

Are you attending a support group as you work through this journal and companion text? ☐ Yes ☐ No

If so, can you describe how this group experience is going for you so far?

Are you seeing a grief counselor? ☐ Yes ☐ No

If so, what has the counseling experience been like for you so far?

_____

_____

_____

_____

_____

_____

_____

_____

WHY 4:

Your Unique Personality

What are some adjectives you would use to describe yourself?

_____   _____

_____   _____

_____   _____

_____   _____

_____   _____

_____   _____

_____   _____

_____   _____

How do you think your unique personality is influencing your grief and mourning?

_____

_____

_____

_____

_____

_____

_____

How have you responded to other life losses or crises in your life? Are you responding in a similar way now, or does this loss feel different? Explain.

_____

_____

_____

_____

_____

_____

_____

_____

_____

Do you think your personality has changed as a result of this death? If so, how? If not, why not?

How is your self-esteem right now?

Do you think this death has impacted how you feel about yourself? If so, how?

WHY 5:

The Unique Personality of the Person Who Died

Check off the personality traits that seem to describe the person who died.

☐ accepting	☐ dynamic	☐ overprotective
☐ active	☐ emotional	☐ overwhelming
☐ adventuresome	☐ energetic	☐ perfectionistic
☐ aggressive	☐ enthusiastic	☐ persuasive
☐ annoying	☐ fair	☐ playful
☐ anxious	☐ forgetful	☐ protective
☐ argumentative	☐ friendly	☐ punctual
☐ artistic	☐ funny	☐ quick to anger
☐ big-hearted	☐ good-natured	☐ rebellious
☐ calm	☐ graceful	☐ resourceful
☐ caring	☐ honest	☐ rude
☐ charming	☐ hyperactive	☐ romantic
☐ clever	☐ imaginative	☐ scatterbrained
☐ cold	☐ independent	☐ self-centered
☐ compassionate	☐ inflexible	☐ sensitive
☐ competitive	☐ influential	☐ shy
☐ conceited	☐ insecure	☐ sincere
☐ confident	☐ interesting	☐ smart
☐ controlling	☐ inventive	☐ spiritual
☐ cooperative	☐ irritable	☐ spontaneous
☐ courageous	☐ jealous	☐ stubborn
☐ creative	☐ logical	☐ temperamental
☐ critical	☐ loud	☐ tireless
☐ demanding	☐ moody	☐ troubled
☐ dependable	☐ nervous	☐ trustworthy
☐ detached	☐ nurturing	☐ two-faced
☐ direct	☐ opinionated	☐ warm
☐ dramatic	☐ outgoing	☐ wise

Now, in your own words, describe the personality of the person who died.

Place a photo of the person who died here—one you think expresses their unique personality. Or if you're so inclined, draw the person.

What roles did this person play in your life? (For example, husband, best friend, advisor, lover, playmate, anchor, etc.)

How did this person's unique personality affect the roles they played in your life?

What personality traits of this person did you enjoy the most?

Give an example of a time when these personality traits really shone through in this person.

_____

_____

_____

_____

_____

_____

_____

_____

_____

_____

What personality traits of this person did you least enjoy?

_____

_____

_____

_____

_____

_____

_____

_____

_____

Give an example of a time when these negative traits were apparent to you.

If you were asked to list the three personality traits you admired the most in this person, what would those be? (You might want to review the checklist on p. 65.)

WHY 6:
Your Cultural Background

What is your cultural background?

How does this background influence your grief and mourning?

If you were asked to articulate them, what would you say some of your family of origin's "rules" were about coping with loss and grief? In what ways did you see these rules carried out?

How do you feel about these rules and their helpfulness to you (or unhelpfulness to you) in grief?

WHY 7:

Your Religious or Spiritual Background

Did you grow up with certain religious or spiritual teachings? Please describe them.

Have your religious or spiritual beliefs changed over time? If so, describe how they have changed.

How has this death affected your belief system or spirituality? Be specific.

Do you have people around you who understand and support you in your faith or spirituality? If so, who are these people, and how can they help you now?

Do you think that your faith, religion, or spiritual background is playing a part in your healing process? Please explain.

WHY 8:

Other Crises or Stresses in Your Life Right Now

What other stresses or crises are a part of your life right now?

How are they affecting your grief?

What other losses have come about in your life either as a result of the death or coincidentally during the same time frame?

How do you see these other losses influencing your grief?

Whom can you turn to right now to help you cope with these ripple-effect losses or concurrent stresses?

WHY 9:

Your Experiences with Loss and Death in the Past

Have you had other significant death losses in your life? If so, please describe them.

Compared to these previous grief journeys, how does this grief journey feel for you and why?

Have you experienced any significant non-death losses in your life, such as divorce, health issues, job loss, etc? If so, write them down and consider how they might now be affecting your grief.

WHY 10:

Your Physical and Mental Health

Were you having physical or mental health challenges before the death? If so, please describe them.

How have your physical and mental health been since the death?

WHY 11:

Your Gender

Do you think that that cultural expectations about gender have affected your grief and mourning? If so, how? If not, why not?

Have gender constructs influenced how other people support you in your grief? If so, how?

Do you have any questions, concerns, or frustrations about how gender issues may be influencing your grief journey? Please write them down here. Also, who could you talk to about them?

WHY 12:

The Ritual or Funeral Experience

Did you plan and/or attend a funeral or memorial service for the person who died? If so, describe what this experience was like for you.

If you were not able to be a part of the service or there was no ceremony, how do you feel about that?

Do you think it would be helpful for you to create an additional ritual to help you and others heal? What ideas do you have for creating such a ceremony?

In what ways could you continue to use ceremony to honor the person who died at other special times, such as their birthday or the anniversary of their death?

OTHER WHYS

Are there other factors, large or small, that are influencing your grief right now? If so, write about them here.

Explore Your Feelings of Loss

In this chapter in the companion text...

We acknowledged that as strange as your emotions may seem, they are a true expression of where you are right now in your journey through grief. We emphasized that whatever your grief thoughts and feelings are, they are normal and necessary. Feelings aren't right or wrong, they just are. Acknowledging, naming, and embracing them are the first steps to integrating them and helping them soften over time. It's actually the process of becoming friendly with your feelings that will help you heal.

Before exploring some of your specific feelings about the death of your special person, please take a moment to write out a few words that describe all the things you're feeling right now. Right now, I'm feeling...

SHOCK, NUMBNESS, DENIAL, AND DISBELIEF

Did you feel in shock or numb after the death? Do you still feel these things now? What has this been like for you?

Do you feel your shock and numbness helped you through the early days after the death? If yes, how? If no, why not?

Do you feel that you are or have been in denial about the death at any level? Please explain.

Are you learning to allow yourself to acknowledge the death in small doses in between periods of denial? In the companion book, I called this normal back-and-forth evade—encounter. If you tend to get stuck on evade, how could you help yourself better encounter the reality of the death and your grief?

How have your feelings of shock, numbness, denial, and disbelief changed or softened since the death?

What are you doing to express your feelings of shock, numbness, denial, and disbelief?

DISORGANIZATION, CONFUSION, SEARCHING, AND YEARNING

In the companion book, I explained that you may feel a sense of restlessness, agitation, impatience, and ongoing confusion. Have you felt these feelings, and if so, what have they been like for you?

Do you keep starting tasks but never finishing them? Do you forget what you're saying mid-sentence? Are you having trouble getting through your day-to-day commitments? Name some ways your normal grief feelings of disorganization and confusion are affecting your life.

Have you experienced a yearning or searching for the person who died? Please explain.

_____

_____

_____

_____

_____

_____

Do you think you've "seen" or "heard" the person who died? If so, write about this experience.

_____

_____

_____

_____

_____

Do you dream about the person who died? Describe your dreams.

_____

_____

_____

_____

_____

What are you doing to express your feelings of disorganization, confusion, searching, and yearning?

ANXIETY, PANIC, AND FEAR

Have you felt anxious, panicked, or fearful since the death? If so, please explain.

What are you most afraid of since the death?

What are you doing to express your feelings of anxiety, panic, and fear?

In the space below, write out what you are doing, or have done, to help yourself with feelings of anxiety, panic, and fear.

EXPLOSIVE EMOTIONS

Have you felt anger, hate, blame, terror, resentment, rage, and/or jealousy about the death or since the death? If not, write about why you think these feelings haven't been a part of your grief journey so far. If so, which of these feelings have you experienced? List them below in the left column, then write more about them in the right column.

Have others around you been upset by your expression of these explosive emotions?

What are you doing to express your explosive emotions in healthy ways?

GUILT AND REGRET

Have you had a case of the "if-onlys" since the death? If so, write about them and how they make you feel.

Have you experienced any of the following specific subtypes of guilt? I invite you to check those that apply to you, if any, and write about them below.

☐ Survivor guilt   ☐ Relief-guilt   ☐ Joy-guilt
☐ Magical thinking and guilt   ☐ Longstanding personality factors

How do other people make you feel about your feelings of guilt and regret?

_____

_____

_____

_____

_____

_____

_____

_____

_____

What are you doing to express your guilt and regret?

_____

_____

_____

_____

_____

_____

_____

_____

_____

_____

_____

SADNESS AND DEPRESSION

How sad are you feeling about the death right now? How does this compare to the sadness you may have felt earlier in your grief journey?

Are there certain days or times of day, places, or situations that are saddest for you now? Explain.

When you start feeling sad, what can you do to help yourself embrace your sadness (in doses) instead of turning away from it?

Have you had any thoughts of dying or suicide since the death? If so, please explain.

Keep in mind than when experiencing grief, passive thoughts of dying are normal, but active thoughts of suicide are not. If you are actively considering or making plans to take your own life, put down this journal this very moment and call someone who will help you get help. If this is an emergency, call 911 immediately.

What are you doing to express your sadness and natural depression?

_____

_____

_____

_____

_____

_____

_____

_____

_____

_____

_____

_____

CLINICAL DEPRESSION

Do you think you might be clinically depressed? If yes, please review the chart on page 87 in the companion book and see if you meet any of the criteria for clinical depression. If you do or might, in the space below write down your primary-care provider's name and phone number then put down this journal, pick up your phone, and make an appointment to see them as soon as possible. Remember that getting help for clinical depression does not mean you are weak—it means you are strong.

Provider name _____

Provider phone number _____

RELIEF AND RELEASE

Did you feel a sense of relief or release after the death? If yes, why?

How do you feel about your feelings of relief or release? Do you think they're OK or not OK?

What are you doing to express your feelings of relief and release?

OTHER FEELINGS

Are you having other feelings that haven't been covered in this chapter? Please take a few minutes to explain them here.

Understand the
Six Needs of Mourning

In this chapter in the companion text...

We introduced the six needs of mourning, which are the six central needs that all mourners must meet—over time and with the support of others—in order to heal. Unlike the concept of "stages" of grief, the six needs are not orderly or predictable. You will probably jump around in random fashion while working on them, you may often experience more than one at a time, and you will address each need only when you are ready to do so.

MOURNING NEED 1:

Acknowledge the Reality of the Death

Right now, where do you see yourself in acknowledging the reality of this death?

Do you think the passage of time is playing a part in where you are with this need? If so, how?

Do you understand and allow yourself the need to sometimes push parts of the reality away?

What can you do to continue to work on this need?

MOURNING NEED 2:
Embrace the Pain of the Loss

Where do you see yourself in allowing yourself to feel the pain of the loss?

Do you think the passage of time is playing a part in where you are with this need? If so, how?

With whom have you shared your feelings of hurt?

_____

_____

_____

_____

_____

_____

Write about what sharing your painful feelings has been like for you.

_____

_____

_____

_____

_____

_____

What can you do to continue to work on this need?

_____

_____

_____

_____

_____

_____

_____

MOURNING NEED 3:
Remember the Person Who Died

If you have another favorite picture of the person who died, memento, scrap of fabric, or any other flat item that reminds you of them, place it here in your journal:

Where do you see yourself in the process of remembering the person who died?

Write out below a meaningful story about the person who died.

What do you miss the very most about the person who died?

What do you miss the least about the person who died?

What other things will you always remember about the person who died?

_____

_____

_____

_____

_____

_____

_____

_____

What would you want others to always remember about the person who died?

_____

_____

_____

_____

_____

_____

_____

_____

_____

_____

Can you recount a funny story about the person who died?

_____

_____

_____

_____

_____

_____

_____

_____

A time the person who died encouraged or uplifted me was...

_____

_____

_____

_____

_____

_____

_____

_____

Other ways the person who died was a significant part of my life were...

Things the person who died used to say were...

The most important thing I learned from the person who died was...

In the space below, write a letter to the person who died. Tell them what is on your mind and in your heart.

Dear _____,

In the space below, imagine the person who died could write a letter back to you. What do you think they would want to say to you?

Dear ....,

_____

_____

_____

_____

_____

_____

_____

_____

_____

_____

_____

_____

_____

What can you do to continue to work on this need?

_____

_____

_____

_____

MOURNING NEED 4:
Develop a New Self-Identity

Where do you see yourself right now in the process of developing a new self-identity?

What roles did the person who died play in your life?

What identity changes have you experienced as a result of this death?

_____

_____

_____

_____

_____

_____

_____

_____

How do you see people treating you differently as a result of your changing identity?

_____

_____

_____

_____

_____

_____

_____

_____

_____

Which, if any, positive changes in your self-identity have you noticed since the death?

_____

_____

_____

_____

_____

_____

_____

_____

_____

_____

_____

What can you do to continue to work on this need?

_____

_____

_____

_____

_____

_____

_____

TURNING TO RITUAL TO FACILITATE MOURNING

Death transforms love into grief, and ritual helps transform grief into healing…and more love.

Have you used any group or personal grief rituals as you've been grieving this death? If so, how did they feel while you were doing them, and how did they affect your grief in the days and weeks afterward? Please explain.

Write down any ideas you have for additional personal or group rituals in the weeks and months to come. Give special thought to any upcoming pertinent special days, such as birthday, anniversaries, etc.

MOURNING NEED 5:

Search for Meaning

Where do you see yourself in your search for meaning right now?

Do you have any "Why?" or "How?" questions right now? If so, what are they?

Are you wrestling with your faith or spirituality at the moment?
Explain.

What can you do to continue to work on this need?

Studies have shown that prayer and spiritual time can help people heal. If you believe in a higher power, the space below is provided for you to write out a prayer. You might pray about the person who died or about your questions about life, death, grief, and pain. If your beliefs are more generally spiritual, you can use this space to express your spiritual intentions or aspirations.

MOURNING NEED 6:

Let Others Help You—Now and Always

Where do you see yourself in letting others help you with your grief?

Who has helped you?

What do these people do that lets you know they are there to support you?

How are you doing at accepting support from people who try to give it?

Are you getting support from others who have also experienced the death of someone loved? Please explain.

What can you do to continue to work on this need?

Recognize You Are Not Crazy

In this chapter in the companion text...

We discussed the common feeling people in grief have that they are going crazy. Many of the thoughts and feelings you will experience in your journey through grief are so different from your everyday reality that you may feel you're going crazy. You're not. You're just grieving. The two can feel remarkably similar sometimes. This chapter also explores a number of typical experiences that contribute to the feeling of going crazy in grief.

TIME DISTORTION

Has time seemed distorted to you since the death? Explain.

SELF-FOCUS

Have you felt the need to focus more on yourself and less on others in your journey through grief? Explain.

RETHINKING AND RETELLING YOUR STORY

Do you find yourself thinking about or telling the story of the death over and over again? If so, what is it exactly that you are feeling the need to think and/or talk about? Describe it here.

SUDDEN CHANGES IN MOOD

Have you been moody since the death? Please explain.

POWERLESSNESS AND HELPLESSNESS

Has this death made you feel powerless or helpless? In what ways?

GRIEF ATTACKS OR GRIEFBURSTS

Have you had any griefbursts since the death? If yes, describe where you were and what happened.

CRYING AND SOBBING

Do you find yourself expressing your grief by crying sometimes? If so, how do you feel each time after you're done crying? If not, why do you think you're not crying?

_____

_____

_____

_____

_____

_____

_____

LINKING OBJECTS

Do you have any linking objects that belonged to or remind you of the person who died? If yes, list them here and describe how having them nearby makes you feel. If not, why not?

_____

_____

_____

_____

_____

_____

_____

_____

IDENTIFICATION SYMPTOMS OF PHYSICAL ILLNESS

Have you found yourself experiencing any physical symptoms similar to those of the person who died? If yes, describe them and explain how you feel about these symptoms.

Would it make you feel better to see a physician about these symptoms? If yes, call your physician for an appointment right now and note the time and date of the appointment here.

SUICIDAL THOUGHTS

Have you contemplated suicide since the death? If yes, write about your thoughts here. Also please see page 99 of this journal for more on suicidal thoughts and determining if they are dangerous.

DRUG OR ALCOHOL USE

Have you been using drugs or alcohol to dull your painful feelings of grief? If yes, describe what your use habits have been.

DREAMS

Have you had any pleasant dreams about the person who died? If so, describe them here.

Have you had any unpleasant dreams or nightmares about the person who died? If so, describe them here.

MYSTICAL EXPERIENCES

Have you had any mystical experiences that you believe are some form of communication from the person who died? If yes, write about them and how they made you feel in the space below.

ANNIVERSARIES, HOLIDAYS, AND SPECIAL OCCASIONS

Have you had a tough time coping on an anniversary, birthday, holiday, or other special day since the death? Write about the experience here.

THE CRAZY THINGS PEOPLE SAY AND DO

What platitudes or oblivious things have others said or written to you since the death? Please share them here.

What hurtful things have others done to you since the death? Please share them here.

Nurture Yourself

In this chapter in the companion text...

We reminded ourselves of the need to be self-nurturing in grief. Remember—self-care fortifies you for your long and challenging grief journey. In taking good care of yourself, in allowing yourself the time and loving attention you need to journey safely and deeply through grief, you prepare the way to find meaning in your continued living. We then explored the five areas in which it is critical to nurture yourself: physical, cognitive, emotional, social, and spiritual.

NURTURE YOURSELF

Before we start to consider, one at a time, how you are doing physically, cognitively, emotionally, socially, and spiritually, let's take a step back and give some thought to how you feel about self-care in general and if/how you have prioritized it in the past.

What are your beliefs and feelings about self-care?

Have you historically been someone who has taken good care of yourself? If so, in what ways? If not, in what ways?

If you're someone who struggles with the idea of devoting time and energy to self-care, do you know people who seem good at taking care of themselves physically, cognitively, emotionally, socially, and spiritually? Write their names below as well as the areas in which they excel. Also, sometime this week consider reaching out to them to learn about their philosophy of self-care and how and why they make it a priority.

NURTURING YOUR WHOLE SELF

In the spaces that follow, write out how you see yourself doing in caring for yourself in each of the five areas of self.

Nurturing Yourself Physically

Is your body letting you know that it feels distressed right now? If so, how?

How are you sleeping?

How are you eating?

Please write about your good and not-so-good physical self-care habits here. Of the Twelve Commandments of Good Health (See page 133 of the companion book), which do you feel you are following right now? Which do you think it would help you to focus more on? Consider picking one of the twelve to devote some attention to this week and also note your plan to do that here.

Tuning Into Your Love Language

What is your preferred love language? What is your secondary love language? How could you communicate to others how they can best help you feel loved and supported?

_____

_____

_____

_____

_____

_____

_____

Nurturing Yourself Cognitively

Has your capacity to think, concentrate, and remember been affected by your grief? If so, how?

_____

_____

_____

_____

_____

_____

_____

_____

How are you doing at living mindfully? Do you have any ideas about how to practice mindfulness?

Now that this person has died, what do you want in life? What is wanted of you? While it will likely take months and years to discover satisfying answers to these questions, write here about your current thoughts about them.

Make a list of goals for the coming year. Be reasonable and compassionate with yourself in determining these goals.

Count your blessings. What do you still have to be thankful for in your life? Make a gratitude list here.

Nurturing Yourself Emotionally

How do you give routinely give attention to your thoughts and feelings in grief?

Do you have physical contact with other human beings? If yes, describe how it makes you feel. If no, why not?

What kinds of music touch your heart and soul? List your favorite artists and types of music here. You might also mention music that was important to the person who died.

DRAW A GRIEF MAP HERE.

Make a circle at the center of the page and label it MY GRIEF. This circle represents your thoughts and feelings since the death. Now draw lines radiating out of this circle and label each line with a thought or feeling that has contributed to your grief. For example, you might write ANGER in a bubble at the end of one line. Next to the word anger, jot down notes about why you are mad. If there's not enough room on this page for your grief map, get a big piece of paper and do it there. Remember—you will not be graded for your artistic abilities. Just draw and scribble!

What gives you pleasure and joy in your life? Write down ten things, then think about how you can incorporate at least one into each day.

1. _____
2. _____
3. _____
4. _____
5. _____
6. _____
7. _____
8. _____
9. _____
10. _____

The Loneliness Of Grief

Have you felt lonely since the death? If so, please write about your loneliness. Also make notes about the ways in which you could reach out to others to help soften your loneliness.

_____

_____

_____

_____

_____

_____

_____

Nurturing Yourself Socially

What has been difficult for you socially since the death, and why?

How are you making an effort to stay connected to other people in your life?

Have your friendships changed since the death? If yes, explain. If no, write about why you think your friends have remained so faithful to you.

Do you think having a "grief buddy"—someone who is also mourning a death that you could partner with in healing—would be helpful to you? If yes, write down the names of a few people you could approach with this idea.

Nurturing Yourself Spiritually

Write about your spiritual journey since the death. What have you struggled with? What has been comforting to you?

How do you nurture your spirit?

Do you have a place where you can grieve and sit in silence, all by yourself? Describe this place.

_____

_____

_____

_____

_____

_____

_____

_____

Do you pray or meditate? Describe your routine here.

_____

_____

_____

_____

_____

_____

_____

_____

_____

_____

Would planting a special tree in honor of the person who died help you and others continue to heal? If yes, call someone today and discuss when and where to plant the tree and what kind of small ceremony you might have. If no, what other ritual might help you honor your grief and remember the person who died?

Do you regularly spend time outdoors? If yes, how does it make you feel? If no, how could you incorporate a little more nature time into your days?

Do you believe in heaven or a possible afterlife of some kind? If you do, close your eyes and imagine the person who died there. What is it like? Write about this image here.

Reach Out for Help

In this chapter in the companion text...

We emphasized that healing in grief requires the support and understanding of those around you as you embrace the pain of your loss. You cannot make this journey alone. You must not only accept the help of others—you must reach out for it. We also discussed reaching out to a support group, reaching out to a grief counselor, and reaching out when your grief is complicated.

In general, how are you at accepting support from others and proactively reaching out when you need help?

List three people you have received support from thus far in your grief journey and describe the ways in which they have (and possibly haven't) helped you:

1. _____

This person has helped me by

_____

_____

_____

_____

_____

2. _____

This person has helped me by

_____

_____

_____

_____

_____

3. _____

This person has helped me by

_____

_____

_____

_____

_____

WHERE TO TURN FOR HELP

Do you have close friends and compassionate family members who are your companions on your journey through grief? If yes, write about who these people are and how they have helped you and will continue to help you. If no, write about where else you might seek support.

Is there a religious or spiritual leader or mentor you could turn to for support? If so, who?

Have you located a support group to attend or professional counselor to see? If so, you'll be asked to describe them later in this journal chapter. If not, explore why you haven't felt the need or desire to seek out a support group or counselor at this time.

THE RULE OF THIRDS

The rule of thirds says that when you're in grief, you'll typically find that about one-third of the people in your life will neither help nor harm you, one-third will be a hindrance to your efforts to heal, and one-third will be good helpers. Below, write about those in the last group.

HOW OTHERS CAN HELP YOU
Who helps you feel hopeful?

Who listens to you talk about your grief and can be compassionately present as you express the pain of your loss?

Who helps you feel, in general, that you are being companioned on your grief journey?

REACHING OUT TO A SUPPORT GROUP
First, write a little about your thoughts, feelings, questions, hopes, and apprehensions about support groups in general.

HOW TO FIND A GRIEF SUPPORT GROUP

Have you looked into grief support group options? If so, write about what you learned here. What are some good resources?

HOW TO KNOW IF YOU'VE FOUND A HELPFUL SUPPORT GROUP

If you're already part of a grief support group, write a little about your group experience here. If you're not, write about if, when, and why you may or may not consider joining a support group.

In what ways is your group helpful? In what ways is it less helpful?

REACHING OUT TO A GRIEF COUNSELOR

First, write a little about your thoughts, feelings, questions, hopes, and apprehensions about the possibility of seeing a grief counselor.

If you've seen a counselor at any point in your life prior to this death, please write about that experience here.

MOURNING CARRIED GRIEF

Has this death brought up previous losses in your life? Do you think you might be carrying old grief that also needs attention and eventual reconciliation? Please write about this here.

HOW TO FIND A GOOD COUNSELOR

If you've looked into finding a grief counselor, write down what you've learned here. If not, make a few notes about the steps you might take to find a grief counselor if and when you realize it would be helpful to you.

If you're already working with a grief counselor, write about what it has been like for you.

LENGTH OF COUNSELING

What are your thoughts, feelings, and questions about how long to see a counselor? Note them here so that if and when you first meet with a counselor, you'll be prepared to discuss this.

Note: If you are severely depressed, considering or planning suicide, or abusing drugs or alcohol, please talk to someone right now about your struggles. You may write about them in this journal, as well, but to help yourself and protect those you love, you must also talk to someone you trust. It is also appropriate to call 911 if your life may be in danger.

REACHING OUT WHEN YOUR GRIEF IS COMPLICATED

Do you think your grief might be extra complicated because of the circumstances of the death, your personality and mental health, your relationship with the person who died, your capacity to express your grief, your use of drugs or alcohol, or other factors? Please write about if and how your grief may or may not be extra complicated.

CATEGORIES OF COMPLICATED GRIEF

Do you recognize yourself in any of the categories of complicated grief? If so, write about them here. Be sure to be gentle and compassionate with yourself. Complicated grief is not a disorder or a failure. It is a normal response to an abnormally complex loss situation.

GETTING HELP FOR COMPLICATED GRIEF

If you think you may be experiencing complicated or traumatic grief, you will likely need a little extra help engaging with and navigating the six needs of mourning. Experienced grief therapists have the training you need. Write down your ideas for finding a good grief therapist in your community.

Seek Reconciliation,
Not Resolution

In this chapter in the companion text...

We defined what it means to reconcile your grief instead of "recovering" from it or "resolving" it. We explained that as the experience of reconciliation unfolds, you will recognize that life is and will continue to be different without the presence of the person who died. Yet you will also move forward in life with a renewed sense of energy and confidence, an ability to fully acknowledge the reality of the death, and a capacity to become reinvolved in the activities of living. We also listed a number of "signs" that reconciliation is taking place in your journey. We cautioned about managing your expectations and not being too attached to outcome. Finally, we explored the role of continued hope and faith in your journey toward reconciliation.

In the space below, take the opportunity to write out where you see yourself in your own unique healing process right now. As you have learned about the concept of reconciliation, what thoughts and feelings have come to mind? Be compassionate and patient with yourself if you are not as far along in your healing as you (or others) would like. After all, through reading *Understanding Your Grief* and completing this journal, you have certainly created some divine momentum toward reconciliation.

What questions, concerns, comments, or fears do you have about reconciling your grief?

SIGNS OF RECONCILIATION

Which, if any, of the Signs of Reconciliation are you noticing in yourself right now? List them here.

Here, write about what you are doing or have done to help yourself move toward reconciliation.

_____

_____

_____

_____

_____

_____

_____

_____

MANAGING YOUR EXPECTATIONS

What were your expectations for healing when you first came to grief? What are they now? What have you learned about the realities of the journey through grief?

_____

_____

_____

_____

_____

_____

_____

_____

_____

Have you consciously or unconsciously given yourself a deadline
to heal? Write about your thoughts and feelings about the duration
of grief.

If you're feeling frustrated, doubtful, or hopeless about your
progress toward healing, what ideas do you have for lessening your
frustrations, easing your doubts, and fostering hope?

NOT ATTACHED TO OUTCOME

What are your thoughts and feelings about the concept of doing the work of mourning while not being attached to outcome?

In your grief journey, what can you control, and what can't you control? Make note of both, then write about letting go of any expectations you might have of items in the second category.

CHOOSING HOPE FOR YOUR HEALING

Do you have hope for your healing? Explain.

What can you do to foster more hope?

BORROWING HOPE

If your hope stores are low, what can you do to borrow some?

THE SAFETY NET OF FAITH

Does your faith sustain you in your journey to reconciliation in grief? What do you have faith in? Explain.

If your faith is a bridge that can help you get from your now to your future, describe the type and condition of your bridge today.

Appreciate Your Transformation

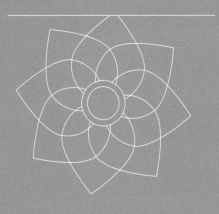

In this chapter in the companion text...

We affirmed that the journey through grief is life-changing and that when you emerge from the wilderness of your grief, you are simply not the same person you were when you entered it. We also recognized that the transformation you may see in yourself—and the personal growth you are experiencing as a result of the death—are not changes you would choose or masochistically seek out. The fact that you are indeed transformed does not mean you are grateful the person died. Still, we explored the various ways in which people grow through grief. We also asked you to consider how you can most authentically and fully live your transformed life from here forward.

So far, how are you discovering that you are being transformed by your grief?

CHANGE IS GROWTH

What changes have you seen in yourself (new attitudes, insights, skills) since the death?

BEFRIENDING IMPERMANENCE IS GROWTH

How are you doing with acknowledging and befriending the impermanence of all things in life?

FINDING A NEW NORMAL IS GROWTH

How has your normal shifted and changed since the death? What are your hopes and intentions for your new normal in the months and years to come?

EXPLORING YOUR ASSUMPTIONS ABOUT LIFE IS GROWTH

Have your values, priorities, and assumptions changed since the death? If so, how?

Have your spiritual beliefs and assumptions changed? If so, how?

EMBRACING VULNERABILILTY IS GROWTH

How are you at allowing yourself to be vulnerable? Are you opening yourself to more vulnerability since the death? Please explain your changing relationship with vulnerability.

LEARNING TO USE YOUR POTENTIAL IS GROWTH

Do you believe you have a purpose in life? If so, what is it? If not, why not?

What are some of the ways you are learning to use your potential?

YOUR RESPONSIBILITY TO LIVE

Do you agree that your life is a precious gift and that you have a responsibility to fully live it? Why or why not?

Do you believe that you have a responsibility to live, in part, on behalf of the person who died? If yes, why? If no, why not?

What could you do in your present and future life to honor the life of the person who died?

Name one specific thing you could do today to honor the person's unfinished contributions to the world:

NOURISHING YOUR TRANSFORMED SOUL

How do you nourish your grieving soul? List the ways here.

How will you most authentically live your transformed life?

Continuing
Your Journey

In the months and years to come, I invite you to revisit this book and reflect on the ongoing and ever-changing nature of your journey through grief. How is your grief changing? How do you know you are getting closer to reconciliation in your grief? In what ways do you see yourself continuing to transform? Please take a moment now and then to jot down updates in the blank pages that follow. Thank you so much for making such good use of this journal to engage your grief and allow yourself to authentically mourn.

I hope we meet one day.

UNDERSTANDING
YOUR

Grief

TEN ESSENTIAL TOUCHSTONES
FOR FINDING HOPE AND
HEALING YOUR HEART
(SECOND EDITION)

ALAN D. WOLFELT, PH.D

Understanding Your Grief

Since its debut in 1992, this favorite by one of the world's most beloved grief counselors has found a place in the homes and hearts of hundreds of thousands of mourners across the globe. Filled with compassion and hope, *Understanding Your Grief* helps you understand and befriend your painful, complex, yet normal thoughts and feelings after the death of someone loved.

Understanding Your Grief is built on Dr. Wolfelt's Ten Touchstones—basic principles to learn and actions to take to help yourself engage with your grief and create momentum toward healing. This second edition includes concise additional wisdom on new topics such as the myth of closure, complicated and traumatic grief, grief overload, loneliness, the power of ritual, and more. Excellent as an empathetic handbook for anyone in mourning as well as a text for support groups, *Understanding Your Grief* also pairs with *The Understanding Your Grief Journal*.

If you're grieving a death or a significant loss of any kind, this refreshed bestseller will be your rock and steadfast companion as you journey through the wilderness of your unique grief.

ISBN 978-1-61722-307-5 • 215 pages • softcover • $14.95

ALL DR. WOLFELT'S PUBLICATIONS CAN BE ORDERED BY MAIL FROM:

Companion Press | 3735 Broken Bow Road | Fort Collins, CO 80526

(970) 226-6050 | www.centerforloss.com

ALSO IN THE *UNDERSTANDING YOUR GRIEF* SERIES

The Understanding Your Grief Support Group Guide

When we're grieving the death of someone loved, we need the support and compassion of our fellow human beings. Grief support groups provide a wonderful opportunity for this very healing kind of support.

This book is for professional or lay caregivers who want to start and lead an effective grief support group for adults. It explains how to get a group started and how to keep it running smoothly once it's underway. The group leader's roles and responsibilities are explored in detail.

This Guide also includes twelve meeting plans that interface with the second editions of *Understanding Your Grief* and *The Understanding Your Grief Journal.* Each week group members read a chapter in the main text, complete a chapter in the journal, and come to group ready for you to guide them through an exploration of the content followed by open discussion.

ISBN: 978-1-617223-11-2 • 131 pages • softcover • $19.95

ALL DR. WOLFELT'S PUBLICATIONS CAN BE ORDERED BY MAIL FROM:

Companion Press | 3735 Broken Bow Road | Fort Collins, CO 80526

(970) 226-6050 | www.centerforloss.com

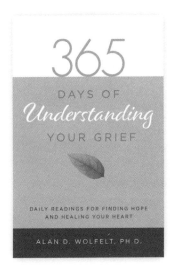

365 Days of Understanding Your Grief

After a significant loss, grief is an everyday experience. But through conscious reflection each day, you can remind yourself that grief, while painful, is a normal, necessary part of your love for the person who died.

Those who grieve will find comfort and understanding in this daily companion. These one-page-a-day readings will help you feel supported and encouraged to mourn well so you can go on to live well and love well. Written as a companion to his classic title *Understanding Your Grief,* this gem can be read in concert or as a standalone book. As you engage with the regular doses of guidance, you will discover reflections that invite you to relight your divine spark.

Reading just one page each day will help you sustain hope and heal your broken heart. For the next year, allow this little book to be your steadfast support and companion.

ISBN: 978-1-61722-299-3 • 384 pages • softcover • $14.95

ALL DR. WOLFELT'S PUBLICATIONS CAN BE ORDERED BY MAIL FROM:

Companion Press | 3735 Broken Bow Road | Fort Collins, CO 80526

(970) 226-6050 | www.centerforloss.com